MW01600864

Atomic Christianity

for Gen Zers

Randy Short

© 2025

Title: Atomic Christianity, for Gen Zers

Author: Randy Short
© 2025

All references and quotations of the Bible are taken from
the ESV® Bible (The Holy Bible, English Standard
Version®), © 2001 by Crossway, a publishing ministry of
Good News Publishers. ESV Text Edition: 2025.

All rights reserved. No part of this book may be
reproduced or transmitted in any form or by any means,
electronic or mechanical, including photocopying,
recording, or any information storage system, without the
written permission of the author.

ISBN: 9798275439021

Table Contents

DEDICATION

I dedicate this book to Edward C. Wharton, a beloved teacher who passed away recently. In fact, I have suggested reading a couple of the books he authored in this edition.

INTRODUCTION

We were already seeing Gen Zers becoming more conservative; some going to church and reading their Bibles. The Wall Street Journal reported in September of 2025 that there was a 36% jump in Bible sales compared to a year earlier. That was after the assignation of Charlie Kirk. Now even more of you are picking up Bibles, reading them and are ready to obey. My hope is that all Gen Zers continue to do just that.

My hope is also that you become the influencers and not the influenced by the traditional conflicting teachings of the many churches. Accept the Bible in its simplicity as the path we should all follow. We have had enough division in Christianity over these 2,000 years. We need to be united in the simple message of the Bible. That is a message for all generations. Division is sinful. Unity of all disciples is what Jesus wanted. United we stand and divided we fall is not just a cute saying. It is a Biblical principal.

Jesus called for the unity of all disciples

> **John 17:20** I do not pray for these alone, but also for those who will believe in Me through their word; 21 that they all may be one, as You, Father, are in Me, and I in You; that they also may

be one in Us, that the world may believe that You sent Me.

Jesus' prayer was not just for his disciples who were present with Him at the time. He prayed for all of us who believe in Him through those disciples' words. He set the bar extremely high. He said we should be united like He and His Father are united. That means it requires effort on our part. We should not just choose a Christian tradition to follow but rather seek out the unifying message He left us in the Bible.

The apostle Paul thought equally about the need for unity.

> **1 Corinthians 1:10** Now I plead with you, brethren, by the name of our Lord Jesus Christ, that you all speak the same thing, and that there be no divisions among you, but that you be perfectly joined together in the same mind and in the same judgment.

Paul does not lower the bar Jesus set. He pleads for unity in the name of Jesus. If we suppose to know the will of God for our lives and for the church beyond what the Bible clearly teaches, we will only become more divided.

The Bible unites people by providing a common foundation of faith in Jesus Christ. Without that common ground how can opinionated human beings ever be united? Human traditions held by many churches divide. The Bible unites.

The Bible created a shared belief system. It has a unified story from Genesis to Revelation. It has a single set of core beliefs, such as one Lord, one faith, and one baptism.

The Bible teaches that through Christ, believers are united to God and to one another. Once saved we become part of the "one body of Christ", the church.

The Bible encourages believers to act in unity through love, harmony, and forgiveness. We are to "put off our old self" and live a new life in Christ.

The Bible's message of unity is spiritual and supersedes human differences in economic status, culture, race, or background. Someone may ask why did Jesus die on the cross and the most common answer is to save humankind. That is true and so important. There is however another important reason for His death that is seldom mentioned. The apostle Paul put it this way.

> **Ephesians 2:16** and that He might reconcile them both to God in one body through the cross, thereby putting to death the enmity. 17 And He came and preached peace to you who were afar off

and to those who were near. 18 For through Him
we both have access by one Spirit to the Father

When Paul says "them both" a study of the context will
show you that he means both Jews and Gentiles. Gentile
means any person who is not Jewish. The term is of Latin
origin and means "of the same clan, family, or nation."
Early Christians used this word to translate the Hebrew
word for "nations". For the Jews in that age, it was us or
them. The nation of Israel or the nations. Paul was saying
that Jesus died on the cross to unite all people. There is
no us and them in the spiritual realm. There is only us.
Let us put forth an effort in this new wave of enthusiasm
for Jesus to be what he wants us to be, among other things,
united.

Chapter 1
God Exists

Genesis 1:1 "In the beginning, God created the heavens and the earth."

This single verse stands as one of the most profound declarations in all of Scripture. It begins not with an argument or explanation for God, but with the affirmation: God exists. He is the Creator of everything. The Bible opens not with a defense of God's reality but with the assertion of His creative authority. For believers, this statement provides the foundation upon which all truth, meaning, and morality rest. Do you believe in God?

In every generation, humanity has wrestled with the question of origins. Does God truly exist? Is belief in God a relic of the past? Can reason, science, and philosophy explain the universe without belief in a divine Creator? The conclusions we reach significantly influence our worldview.

From a Christian apologetic perspective, the statement that "atheism requires more faith than Christianity" is not meant as an insult to anyone. It is just saying that Christian faith is at the minimum a rational faith and supported by evidence just as much if not more so than the common scientific teachings today. It also affirms that though science tries to explain the origin of the universe and the origin of life through empirical evidence, much of what it stands on is not empirical at all.

The scientific method cannot be used to answer the question of origins. The scientific method is a systematic process for investigating phenomena and answering questions through observation and experimentation. It involves seeing and forming a testable hypothesis, designing, and conducting experiments to test the hypothesis, analyzing the results, and drawing conclusions. That is impossible when it comes to origins. Without the ability of observing the origins, we are left with blind faith. Science, when it comes to origins is blind. Christianity invites people not to blind belief but to reasoned trust in a God who has revealed Himself in creation, conscience, the Bible, and the Christ of the Bible.

Atheism must account for the existence of the universe without reference to a Creator. The atheist explanation relies on naturalistic processes. Space, time, matter, and energy came into existence through purely natural causes. Perhaps everything emerged from nothing. Perhaps everything emerged from some quantum fluctuation. Those things are not provable and from the Christian viewpoint, demand a kind of faith. They have a conviction that the universe created itself or that something came from nothing without cause or intention.

The Christian explanation is vastly different. It is that an infinite, intelligent, and personal God created the universe and is the origin of life. This aligns with both philosophical reasoning and the evidence of design seen throughout nature. Every law of physics, every complex biological system, and every order of life reflects the hand of a Designer. The universe's fine-tuning for life, its mathematical precision, our moral code and all the beauty we see around us point to a Creator God.

> Genesis 1:1 is not as a myth but as the most rational starting point of all: In the beginning, God.

The Question of Meaning and Purpose

If there is no God, then life ultimately has no inherent meaning or purpose beyond what individuals or societies choose to assign it. From a purely atheistic worldview, humanity is the product of chance. We are temporary beings in a purposeless universe. To accept this conclusion requires remarkable faith. This viewpoint contradicts the universal human longing for significance, love, and beauty.

> So God created man in his own image, in the image of God he created him; male and female he created them. Genesis 1:27

The Christian worldview, on the other hand, offers a profound and fulfilling answer to what our purpose is. Human life has meaning because it originates from a Creator who made us in His image and for His purpose. Every human being possesses dignity, value, and worth not because of social convention and even less so because of evolution. We possess value because we are the workmanship of God. Believers find meaning not in random existence but in relationship with God and one another. Our purpose flows from participating in God's plan for creation, redemption, and eternal fellowship.

The Question of Morality

Speaking to an atheistic believer in the scientific explanation for the origin of the universe and life Charlie Kirk said:

> "I would argue you have a lot more faith than I do. You have a lot more blind faith to believe that everything around you, love, joy, peace, sadness, is all just a construct of neurons firing in your brain."

Morality presents another challenge for a purely naturalistic worldview. If God does not exist, moral values and duties must arise from human agreement, biology, or cultural evolution. Yet such foundations are unstable. If morality is merely a product of evolution or society, it becomes subjective. What one society praises, another may condemn. There would be no ultimate right or wrong. That leaves us with morality being only an agreed to preference or a strategy for survival.

Christianity, however, grounds morality in the very nature of God. God is good, just, loving, and righteous. Our moral awareness reflects the moral image of our Creator. The existence of a transcendent moral law points to a moral lawgiver. This provides not only a stable foundation for morality and ethics but also a source of hope and accountability.

The moral argument for God's existence is not a threat to human autonomy but a testimony to the divine imprint within us. It is a reminder that we were made to know and reflect God's goodness.

The Nature of Biblical Faith

Many skeptics define faith as "belief without evidence." Yet, the biblical concept of faith is far richer. The Greek word pistis means trust or confidence. It is faith that rests upon knowledge and evidence. Christian faith is not blind. It is a reasoned trust based on the character and revelation of God.

Throughout Scripture, God invites people to examine the evidence: the works of His hands in creation.

> **Psalm 19:1** The heavens declare the glory of God; And the firmament shows His handiwork.

> **Romans 1:20** For since the creation of the world His invisible attributes are clearly seen, being understood by the things that are made, even His eternal power and Godhead, so that they are without excuse,

The Biblical prophecies fulfilled in Christ are also proof of the reality of God. It might be better used to prove that the Bible is the inspired Word of God. The apostle Peter used this argument. In his sermon on the day of Pentecost he speaks of the prophets foreseeing that day.

> **Acts 2:30** Being therefore a prophet and knowing that God had sworn with an oath to him that he would set one of his descendants on his throne, 31 he foresaw and spoke about the resurrection of the Christ, that he was not abandoned to Hades, nor did his flesh see corruption. 32 This Jesus God raised up, and of that we all are witnesses.

Peter also speaks of witnesses to Jesus' resurrection. The fact that the apostles were witnesses and went to their death proclaiming that Jesus had been resurrected from the dead is powerful evidence of this truth. Who would die for a myth?

There were so many witnesses to the resurrection of Jesus. When Paul says that there were more than 500 he also says most are still alive. It was as if he was saying, 'If you do not believe me, go ask them.'

> **1 Corinthians 15:3** For I delivered to you as of first importance what I also received: that Christ died for our sins in accordance with the Scriptures, 4 that he was buried, that he was raised on the third day in accordance with the Scriptures, 5 and that he appeared to Cephas, then to the twelve. 6 Then he appeared to more than five hundred brothers at one time, most of whom are still alive, though some have fallen asleep. 7 Then he appeared to James, then to all the apostles. 8 Last of all, as to one untimely born, he appeared also to me.

The apostle Paul declared that faith is reasonable.

> **2 Timothy 1:12** I know whom I have believed.

Christian apologists emphasize that belief in God is not an irrational leap but a logical response to the evidence of creation, conscience, Scripture, and history. Biblical faith builds upon reason. Biblical faith never discards evidence.

Conclusion: A Rational and Relational Faith

To say that "atheism requires more faith than Christianity" is not to mock unbelief but to highlight the coherence and depth of the Christian worldview. Atheism must believe in an uncaused universe, a purposeless existence, and subjective morality. Christianity offers an integrated vision of reality that satisfies both the mind and the heart.

"In the beginning, God created the heavens and the earth." This is not just the opening line of the Bible. This is the cornerstone of understanding reality. God's existence is the most reasonable, meaningful, and hopeful explanation for the world we have. Faith in God, then, is not the absence of reason. Christian faith is the conclusion founded on evidence and reason.

Suggested Reading

The Truth About Human Origins by Brad Harrub,
Ph.D. & Bert Thompson, Ph/D.

Does God Exist, Editor - Dave Miller, Ph.D.
Contributors: Kyle Butt, Eric Lyons, Jeff Miller, Dave
Miller

Reasons to Believe by Eric Lyons & Kyle Butt

Convicted: A Scientist Examines the Evidence for
Christianity by Brad Harrub, Ph.D. Focus Press, Inc.

Dinner with Skeptics by Jeff Vines

Out With Doubt by Kyle Butt

Chapter 2
God Has Spoken

Romans 15:4 For whatever was written in former days was written for our instruction, that through endurance and through the encouragement of the Scriptures we might have hope.

"The greatest minds of history have been mesmerized by the Scriptures. -- Isaac Newton, Thomas Aquinas. Isaac Newton wrote more about biblical prophecy than even physics." Charlie Kirk

"Read the Bible every single day. Do what the Bible tells you to do. Tell the people what the Bible says." Charlie Kirk

From the beginning of Scripture, humanity is portrayed as a people spoken to by God. Creation itself begins with divine speech: "And God said..." Genesis 1:3. The Bible, therefore, presents a God who communicates, revealing His character, will, and purpose to humankind through words. This concept of divine revelation — that God has spoken and continues to speak — stands at the very foundation of the Christian faith.

For Christians, the Bible is not merely a collection of ancient writings, but the living Word of God, inspired and preserved through generations. The conviction that "God has spoken" shapes how believers view truth, morality, and the human condition. The Scriptures are seen as both historical testimony and spiritual revelation — a bridge between heaven and earth.

The Bible's Claim to Divine Inspiration

Throughout the Scriptures, divine authorship is repeatedly affirmed. Phrases such as "Thus says the Lord" appear more than two thousand times in the Old Testament, indicating that the prophets did not see themselves as originators of their messages but as messengers of divine truth received directly from God. The apostle Paul further explained this writing:

> All Scripture is God-breathed and is useful for teaching, rebuking, correcting and training in righteousness.
> **2 Timothy 3:16**

This idea of God-breathed (Greek: theopneustos) means that Scripture originates from God Himself. It is, of course, spoken or written through human authors. Christians hold that the Holy Spirit guided these writers in such a way that the final product, the Bible, communicates exactly what God intended.

> And we have the prophetic word more fully confirmed, to which you will do well to pay attention as to a lamp shining in a dark place, until the day dawns and the morning star rises in your hearts, 20 knowing this first of all, that no prophecy of Scripture comes from someone's own interpretation. 21 For no prophecy was ever produced by the will of man, but men spoke from

God as they were carried along by the Holy Spirit. **2 Peter 1:19**

Internal Consistency and Unity

The Bible's composition is remarkable in scope. There are sixty-six books, written by more than forty authors. Among these authors there were shepherds, kings, prophets, fishers, and scholars. They wrote separately over roughly fifteen hundred years and across three continents: Asia, Africa, and Europe. Despite all this diversity, the Bible presents one unified narrative from beginning to end. It is the coherent story of God's plan of redemption for humankind.

From Genesis to Revelation, one can trace a continuous thread of promise, fulfillment, and hope. From the creation of man to the fall of man, the call of Abraham, the coming of the Messiah, and the final restoration of all things it is one unified story. To many believers, this unity amid diversity is itself evidence of divine authorship. The Bible's moral, spiritual, and prophetic coherence transcends what could reasonably be expected from human collaboration alone. Such human collaboration would be impossible over such time and distances.

Fulfilled Prophecy as Evidence

Prophecy plays a vital role in affirming the Bible's divine origin. The Old Testament contains hundreds of predictions that Christians believe were fulfilled in the life and ministry of Jesus Christ. The prophet Micah, for instance, foretold that the Messiah would be born in Bethlehem (**Micah 5:2**). Isaiah prophesied that He would be despised, suffer unjustly, and bear the sins of many (**Isaiah 53**).

For believers, these fulfilled prophecies are more than coincidence. They reveal a God who stands outside of time, declaring "the end from the beginning." **Isaiah 46:10** They show that history unfolds according to God's purpose, not chance.

The Transformative Power of Scripture

Beyond historical and textual evidence, Christians often point to the Bible's transforming influence as one of the strongest testimonies to its divine nature. Across centuries and cultures, the message of the Bible has changed hearts, guided nations, and inspired countless acts of compassion, justice, and faith.

The Bible's teachings on love, forgiveness, humility, and redemption continue to shape personal lives and social institutions. From the abolition of slavery and other humanitarian movements the Bible's moral vision has profoundly impacted human progress.

Hebrews 4:12 The word of God is living and active... discerning the thoughts and intentions of the heart.

Though there are those who blame many of the world's wars and persecutions on Christianity, a closer examination one will find that not to be true. Many of the things done in the name of Christianity were not at all based on Christian values as defined by the Bible. They were done by those who were Christian in name only.

Historical and Textual Reliability

In addition to faith-based convictions, Christians point to the remarkable preservation of biblical texts as evidence that God has safeguarded His Word.

Abundant manuscripts

Over 25,000 partial and complete biblical manuscripts exist today. This is far more than for any other ancient textual work. By comparison, only a few dozen manuscripts from Plato or Homer survive. There are only a few partial texts of the history of Rome and Roman wars. Even being few, they are accepted without question as dependable. Why would anyone question the Bible with so much textual evidence?

Early dating

Some New Testament fragments, like the John Rylands Papyrus (P52), date to within a few decades of the original writings, suggesting that the Gospels and epistles were circulated while eyewitnesses were still alive and could have but did not dispute their accuracy.

Textual consistency

While there are variations among manuscripts, these are typically minor. Most involve spelling or word order. None alters core teaching of the Bible.

This wealth of evidence gives scholars high confidence that the Bible we read today reflects accurately the original texts penned by its authors.

Archaeological Corroboration

Archaeological discoveries have also provided valuable historical and geographical context for the Bible. Cities once thought to be mythical such as Nineveh, Jericho, and Ur have been unearthed. The Tel Dan Stele references the "House of David," and the Pilate Stone confirms the Roman governor mentioned in the Gospels.

There are even entire civilizations once thought to be the invention of biblical writers such as the Hittites. Uriah the Hittite mentioned in **2 Samuel 11, 23:39.** Ahimelech the Hittite mentioned in **1 Samuel 26:6.** The Hittites were mentioned also in the time of Solomon as being a significant power in northern Syria. **1 Kings 10:28-29.** The Bible has many references to this people though nothing was known of them outside the Bible. Archeologists did not believe in the existence of this nation until about 1833 when the Hittite capital Hattusa started to be unearthed. There were subsequent discoveries in the beginning of the 19th century quickly putting an end to the doubts that had been raised. The Bible was right.

While archaeology cannot prove miracles or divine activity, it can affirm that many biblical narratives are set in verifiable historical frameworks. Even secular archaeologists often acknowledge that the Bible remains a dependable guide to the ancient Near East.

The Limits of Proof and the Role of Faith

Belief in divine inspiration ultimately rests on faith. Secular historians may accept the Bible's historical value but reject its supernatural claims. Critics point out that citing Scripture as proof of its own authority can be circular reasoning, and that archaeology cannot confirm spiritual truths or miracles.

For the believer, the power of the Bible is not confined to academic validation. The Christian conviction that "God has spoken" is not merely an intellectual position. It is a relationship of trust. Faith accepts that God's revelation, though sometimes beyond human comprehension, is true and life giving.

Conclusion: A Word That Still Speaks

God has indeed spoken, and he continues to speak to us today. The Bible is not a silent relic of history but a living message that addresses every generation. Through the Bible, God comforts the weary, convicts the sinner, and calls humanity to be reconciled with Himself.

As Isaiah wrote,

> The grass withers, the flower fades, but the word of our God will stand forever. **Isaiah 40:8**

The voice that spoke the universe into existence still speaks. He speaks through the Bible to all who will listen.

"I believe in the Bible, and I believe that Christ rose from the dead on the third day. This is the foundation of my faith and guides my actions." Charlie Kirk

Suggested Reading

Apologetics: Evidence for the Bible by Ted Stewart

Apologetics 2: New Discoveries That Confirm the Bible by Ted Stewart

Historical Christian Evidences by Edward C. Wharton

Chapter 3
God Loves Us

John 3:16 For God so loved the world that he gave his only Son, that whoever believes in him should not perish but have eternal life.

"Love is not affirmation, love is not confirmation, love is making sure you care so much about the other that you are willing to challenge and point out flaws when you see them, and have the courage to articulate it, that's what love is." Charlie Kirk

The message of the Bible can be summarized in one word: love. From Genesis to Revelation, God's actions toward humanity are motivated by His divine love. That love is a love that creates, sustains, forgives, and redeems. It is the central truth of the Christian faith.

> **1 John 4:8** Anyone who does not love does not know God, because God is love.

Everything He has done from creating the universe to sending His Son flows from that unchanging nature: love.

Human love, though powerful, is often limited and conditional. God's love, by contrast, is infinite, steadfast, and self-giving. It reaches every person, regardless of background or worthiness. The story of redemption is, at its heart, the story of a God who loves without measure and who acts to restore what has been lost.

The Universal and Benevolent Love of God

The Bible repeatedly emphasizes that God's love extends to all creation. It is not confined by nationality, morality, or merit. This universal love reveals God's goodness and compassion even toward those who do not acknowledge Him.

For the world

> **John 3:16** For God so loved the world,[a] that he gave his only Son, that whoever believes in him should not perish but have eternal life.

The "world" here represents the whole of fallen humanity. People were created in His image but estranged from God by sin. God's love is not abstract. God demonstrated His love in giving His Son. All who believe can be restored to eternal life.

For the wicked

Jesus reminded His followers of God's impartial kindness.

> **Matthew 5:45** so that you may be sons of your Father who is in heaven. For he makes his sun rise on the evil and on the good and sends rain on the just and on the unjust.

God provides for all, even those who oppose Him. This is a testimony to His patience and mercy.

For all creation

> **Psalm 145:9** The Lord is good to all, and his mercy is over all that he has made.

God's benevolent love is not limited to humanity alone but encompasses the natural world. Creation itself flourishes under His care.

An everlasting love

God's love is not a temporary emotion but an eternal commitment.

> **Jeremiah 31:3** the Lord appeared to him from far away. I have loved you with an everlasting love; therefore I have continued my faithfulness to you.

His love endures when all else fades. Even when people rebel or forget Him, God's heart remains open. His love is unearned, offered freely, and revealed in countless acts of providence, patience, and grace.

Conditional and Redemptive Love

While God's benevolent love extends to all, Scripture also

reveals a redemptive love. It is a deeper, covenantal relationship reserved for those who respond in faith. This love is not limited by God's desire but by human acceptance of His gift.

For sinners

> **Romans 5:8** but God shows his love for us in that while we were still sinners, Christ died for us.

The cross is the ultimate expression of divine love. Divine love is a love that acts on behalf of the underserving.

For His children

> **1 John 3:1** See what kind of love the Father has given to us, that we should be called children of God; and so we are. The reason why the world does not know us is that it did not know him.

Through faith in Christ, believers become members of God's family. This love is intimate, personal, and eternal.

Unconditional yet invitational

God's love is unconditional in that it is offered to all, yet it calls for a response. His forgiveness and salvation are gifts that must be received through repentance and faith.

1 John 4:10 In this is love, not that we have loved God but that he loved us and sent his Son to be the propitiation for our sins.

God's love is both inclusive and transformative. It welcomes all but does not leave anyone unchanged.

Different Perspectives on God's Love

Throughout Christian history, theologians have sought to understand how God's universal and saving love coexist.

The Calvinist view emphasizes that while God loves all creation, He shows a special, saving love only toward "the elect." He loves only those He has chosen to redeem. In this view, God's love is powerful and effectual, ensuring that those He calls will come to faith with no choice on their part.

The Arminian view maintains that God's saving love is extended to every person. Salvation is genuinely available to all who choose and have obedient faith. God desires that none should perish, but He allows human freedom to accept or reject His grace.

Which of these theological positions is Biblical? Which do you choose? Do you have a choice? One of these takes the choice from you. The other gives you the freedom to choose.

Old Testament Foundations of Divine Love

The Old Testament portrays God's love in both personal and covenantal ways. His compassion is evident not only toward Israel but toward all nations.

Compassion for all people

> **Psalm 145:9** The Lord is good to all, and his mercy is over all that he has made.

Covenantal faithfulness

God's enduring love is seen in His commitment to Israel despite their repeated disobedience.

> **Isaiah 54:10** For the mountains may depart and the hills be removed, but my steadfast love shall not depart from you, and my covenant of peace shall not be removed," says the Lord, who has compassion on you.

Hope in hardship.

Even in times of judgment, His love never fails.

> **Lamentations 3:22** The steadfast love of the Lord never ceases; his mercies never come to

an end; 23 they are new every morning; great is
your faithfulness.

These passages reveal a God whose love is both tender
and steadfast. It is a love that disciplines yet restores, that
judges yet forgives.

New Testament Fulfillment of God's Love

In the New Testament, God's love reaches its fullest
expression in the life, death, and resurrection of Jesus
Christ.

The gift of the Son: **John 3:16** declares that divine love is
not passive but sacrificial. God gave His Son — not merely
as a teacher or prophet, but as a Savior who would bear
the sins of the world.

Love for the unworthy

Paul echoes this truth
> **Romans 5:8** but God shows his love for us in
> that while we were still sinners, Christ died for us.

The source of all love

1 John 4:19 We love because he first loved us.

God's love awakens and empowers human love.

The immeasurable depth of divine love

Paul prays that believers might:

> ...have strength to comprehend with all the saints what is the breadth and length and height and depth, and to know the love of Christ that surpasses knowledge, that you may be filled with all the fullness of God. **Ephesians 3:18-19**

It is a love that surpasses knowledge. It is beyond measure or comparison.

Through Jesus, God's love becomes tangible, personal, and transformative. It is no longer an abstract concept, but a living reality experienced in the hearts of those who believe.

The Transforming Power of God's Love

> God's love is to be believed. It is to be experienced. Those who receive His love are called to reflect it in their own lives. Jesus taught that love for God and love for others are the greatest commandments. **Matthew 22:37-39**

This divine love changes everything.
- It transforms fear into faith.
- It replaces guilt with grace.

- It turns enemies into neighbors and strangers into brothers.

When believers grasp the depth of God's love, they find security in His presence and purpose in His call. They begin to see others through His eyes. They see souls as worthy of compassion and redemption.

Conclusion: Love That Never Fails

The love of God is both the starting point and the goal of all Christian belief. It is the heartbeat of the gospel and the foundation of hope. Unlike human affection, which may fade with time or circumstance, God's love endures forever.

As the apostle Paul wrote,

> For I am sure that neither death nor life, nor angels nor rulers, nor things present nor things to come, nor powers, nor height nor depth, nor anything else in all creation, will be able to separate us from the love of God in Christ Jesus our Lord. **Romans 8:38–39**

God's love is a truth to be studied. It is also a relationship to be lived. It reaches down from heaven to draw the human heart upward, inviting all to enter the eternal embrace of the One who first loved us

.

Chapter 4
God Has Great Expectations

John 14:15 If you love me, you will keep my commandments.

Micah 6:8 He has shown you, O mortal, what is good. And what does the Lord require of you? To act justly and to love mercy and to walk humbly with your God.

From Genesis to Revelation, the Bible reveals not only who God is but also what He desires from His people. God's expectations are not arbitrary rules, but the natural response of a heart transformed by His love. Throughout both the Old and New Testaments, His will can be summed up in one simple yet profound truth: God expects His people to live in loving relationship with Him and to reflect His character in the world.

"It is the responsibility of the individual to protect their own freedom and secure their own happiness." Charlie Kirk

The Creator who formed humanity in His image also calls humanity to live in a way that mirrors His holiness, justice, and compassion. These expectations are not burdens but blessings — guiding lights for a life that honors God and blesses others.

God's Expectations in the Old Testament

The Old Testament presents a picture of God's people living
in a covenant relationship with Him. This covenant was not merely legal or ceremonial — it was deeply relational. God called Israel to love, trust, and obey Him, demonstrating their faith through righteous living and compassionate action.

Micah's Summary of God's Will

The prophet Micah beautifully condensed God's moral expectations into three enduring principles:

Act justly

God's people are called to fairness and integrity in all things. This includes honesty in business, compassion in judgment, and protection for the vulnerable (**Exodus 23:1-9**). True justice flows from the recognition that every person bears the image of God.

Love and mercy

Justice without mercy becomes harsh and cold. God's heart is one of compassion and forgiveness. **Psalm 103:8** describes Him as "compassionate and gracious, slow to anger and abounding in love." God's people are expected to reflect that same mercy toward others.

Walk humbly

To walk humbly with God means to live with reverence, gratitude, and submission to His will. It acknowledges that every blessing comes from Him. As James says,

> Humble yourselves before the Lord, and He will lift you up. **James 4:10**

Together, these three actions — justice, mercy, and humility — express what it means to live rightly before God and others.

The Covenant with Israel

The heart of the Old Testament relationship between God and His people is love expressed through obedience.

Loving and obeying God

> You shall therefore love the Lord your God and keep His charge, His statutes, His rules, and His commandments always. **Deuteronomy 11:1**

Obedience is not mere compliance but the overflow of a heart that loves God.

Obedience over sacrifice

God made it clear that outward religious rituals are meaningless without inward devotion. The prophet Samuel told King Saul,

To obey is better than sacrifice. **1 Samuel 15:22**

God desires sincerity over ceremony, relationship over ritual.

In summary, the Old Testament reveals that God's expectations revolve around covenant faithfulness — loving Him wholeheartedly and loving others through justice, mercy, and humility.

God's Expectations in the New Testament

When Jesus came, He did not abolish the Old Testament law but fulfilled and deepened it, **Matthew 5:17**. He revealed the heart behind every command — love.

The Two Greatest Commandments

When asked which commandment was greatest, Jesus summarized the entire law in two statements that define the essence of God's expectations:

Love God

> You shall love the Lord your God with all your heart, with all your soul and with all your mind. **Matthew 22:37–38**

This love is complete. It involves the mind, emotions, and will. It is devotion that shapes every decision and desire.

Love your neighbor

> You shall love your neighbor as yourself. **Matthew 22:39**

Genuine love for God inevitably expresses itself in love for others. Jesus taught that all of Scripture. "the Law and the Prophets" — depends on these two commands **Matthew 22:40**.

Through these teachings, Jesus made clear that love is not only an emotion but an action. God's expectation is that His people demonstrate His love through service, forgiveness, and compassion toward all.

Holiness and Transformation

God not only calls His people to obedience but also

provides the power to live it out. In the New Testament, holiness is no longer achieved through ritual purity but through spiritual transformation.

Holiness in conduct

Believers are called to live lives that reflect God's purity and moral excellence.

> Just as He who called you is holy, so be holy in all you do. **1 Peter 1:15–16.**

Holiness means being distinct from the world — not withdrawn from it but living by a higher standard of love and integrity.

Transformation by the Spirit

God's expectations are fulfilled not by human strength but through the work of the Holy Spirit. Paul describes the Spirit's transforming power in **Galatians 5:22–23**, where the "fruit of the Spirit" — love, joy, peace, patience, kindness, goodness, faithfulness, gentleness, and self-control — replaces the works of the flesh.

The Christian life, therefore, is not about external rule-keeping but internal renewal. God's expectations become attainable as His Spirit changes the believer from within.

The Call to Share God's Love

Another central expectation for God's people is to make His love known to others. Jesus's final command to His followers was not simply to believe but to go and tell.

Making disciples

The mission Jesus gave to all disciples IS:

> Go therefore and make disciples of all nations, baptizing them in the name of the Father and of the Son and of the Holy Spirit, teaching them to observe all that I have commanded you. **Matthew 28:19-20**

Evangelism is not optional but an extension of God's heart for the world.

Witness through action

Jesus taught that love is the believer's greatest testimony.

> By this everyone will know that you are my disciples, if you love one another. **John 13:35**

The way Christians treat others, with kindness, integrity, and compassion, proclaims the gospel more powerfully than words alone. Sharing God's message is both verbal and visible. It preached with the mouth and lived through the heart.

Living as a New Creation

Faith in Christ produces a new beginning. God's expectations for His people are not a return to old laws but a call to live as new creations in Him.

Faith and repentance

A right relationship with God begins with turning from sin and placing faith in Jesus.

> If anyone is in Christ, he is a new creation; the old has gone, the new has come. **2 Corinthians 5:17**.

This spiritual rebirth is the foundation for obedience and transformation.

Glorifying God in all things

The goal of every expectation is that God be glorified. Whether in worship, work, family, or daily living, believers are to reflect His goodness and honor His name.

So, whether you eat or drink or whatever you do, do it all for the glory of God. **1 Corinthians 10:31.**

A life lived for God's glory becomes the truest fulfillment of His expectations. A life lived for God is a living testimony of His grace and power.

Conclusion: A Relationship of Love and Obedience

God's expectations are not meant to burden but to bless. They reveal His character and invite His people into a relationship of trust, obedience, and love. Both the Old and New Testaments affirm that what God truly desires is not empty ritual or outward performance, but a heart that seeks Him.

To act justly, to love mercy, to walk humbly — to love God and love others — these are timeless truths that define the life of faith. In living this way, God's people reflect His light in a dark world and bear witness to the One who calls them His own.

As Jesus said,

> If you love Me, keep My commandments. **John 14:15.**

Love and obedience are inseparable — together they form the heart of what God expects from every believer.

Chapter 5
God's Plan for Your New Life
(the beginning)

Romans 6:4 We were buried therefore with him by baptism into death, in order that, just as Christ was raised from the dead by the glory of the Father, we too might walk in newness of life.

I know that Charlie Kirk said he believed the Bible. I know that he went to church. I do not know how he became a Christian or if it was as the Bible instructs. He did point people in the right direction and asked others to do the same. That direction is found in the Bible.

"You must try to point them toward ultimate purposes and toward getting back to the church, getting back to faith, getting married, having children." Charlie Kirk

Every true believer's story ends and begins again at the same place, the cross of Jesus Christ. From the cross flows the greatest transformation any person can ever experience. You can experience the transition from spiritual death to new life in Christ.

> **John 5:24** Truly, truly, I say to you, whoever hears my word and believes him who sent me has eternal life. He does not come into judgment but has passed from death to life.

This new life is not merely a change of habits or beliefs. It is a complete rebirth of the soul. It is the start of a new existence shaped by God's Spirit, God's grace, and God's purpose.

From the beginning of time God has desired that His creation walk with Him in complete fellowship. Sin broke that fellowship. In His mercy, God designed a perfect plan to restore that fellowship. This plan is revealed in the gospel. Gospel means good news, and it is. Through Jesus Christ, anyone can be forgiven, cleansed, and made new. The apostle Paul called this "newness of life," and it describes a daily walk in the power and peace of knowing that one's past sins are forgiven and one's future is secure in God's hands.

The Bible teaches that this new life begins when a person responds to God's grace through faithful obedience to the gospel. This response follows a simple, yet profound pattern found throughout the New Testament. The pattern to be followed is often simply called the Plan of Salvation. It is not a human invention or a denominational creed. It is the biblical pathway spoken to us by God through His inspired servants and by which one enters a saving relationship with Christ.

God's plan can be summarized in five clear steps that reflect both His love and His justice. Because you are reading this book you may have already taken some of these steps. Each step builds upon the other, leading a sincere heart to forgiveness and a restored relationship with the Creator.

Hear the Gospel

Every journey of faith begins with hearing the Gospel. The word of God awakens the heart to truth and reveals who Jesus is. Faith is not inherited, nor is it born out of emotion. Faith comes from listening to God's revealed word.

> **Romans 10:17** So then faith comes by hearing, and hearing by the word of God.

> **John 8:32** You shall know the truth, and the truth shall make you free.

The message of the cross calls out to every person: God loves you, Christ died for you, and through Him, you can be made whole.

Believe in Jesus Christ

Once the gospel is heard, a choice must be made. Do we believe that Jesus is who He claimed to be? He is the Son of God, the Savior of the world. The Bible tells us so. Do you believe it? Genuine belief is more than intellectual agreement; it is trust that moves the heart to obedience.

> **John 3:16** For God so loved the world that He gave His only begotten Son, that whoever believes in Him should not perish but have everlasting life.

> **John 8:24** Unless you believe that I am He, you will die in your sins.

Belief bridges the gap between hearing and action. It is faith. It is trust. Faith that takes God at His word and reacts positively to it. What should the reaction be?

Repent of Sins

True faith leads to repentance. Repentance is a turning point where one decides to leave behind his or her sinful lifestyle and walk in God's way. Repentance is not merely regret but a complete change of direction. It reflects sorrow for sin and a sincere desire to live according to God's will and acts in sincerity.

> **Acts 17:30** God... now commands all men everywhere to repent

> **Luke 13:3** Unless you repent you will all likewise perish.

Repentance is the doorway to renewal. It opens the heart for God to do His transforming work.

In its essence it is discipleship. A disciple is not just a learner but one who is following Jesus instead of the worldly ways of sin.

> **Luke 9:23** And he said to all, "If anyone would come after me, let him deny himself and take up his cross daily and follow me.

Repenting of the worldly lifestyle and walking with Jesus in His lifestyle is what happens in this essential step.

Confess Faith in Christ

A heart that believes cannot remain silent. Confession is the open acknowledgment that Jesus Christ is Lord. It is a declaration of allegiance and trust. It is a declaration of commitment to Christ and one's intention to fulfill it. It is a public step of faith that affirms the believer's commitment to follow Christ.

> **Romans 10:9–10** If you confess with your mouth the Lord Jesus and believe in your heart that God has raised Him from the dead, you will be saved.

> **Matthew 10:32** Whoever confesses Me before men, him I will also confess before My Father who

50

is in heaven.

Confessing Jesus Christ as Lord means admitting that Jesus is the head of your life, not just as savior of it. All your decisions pass through the filter of His will. You are confessing that you will do only what glorifies your Lord. Your will is subject to his. This confession makes faith visible and lets the world know those to whom we belong.

The Ethiopian Eunuch confessed Jesus though the word Lord was not used. I do believe it is implied. What do you think?

Acts 8:34 And the eunuch said to Philip, "About whom, I ask you, does the prophet say this, about himself or about someone else?" 35 Then Philip opened his mouth, and beginning with this Scripture he told him the good news about Jesus. 36 And as they were going along the road they came to some water, and the eunuch said, "See, here is water! What prevents me from being baptized?" 37: And Philip said, "If you believe with all your heart, you may." And he replied, "I believe that Jesus Christ is the Son of God." 38 And he commanded the chariot to stop, and they both went down into the water, Philip and the eunuch, and he baptized him.

He confessed, "I believe that Jesus Christ is the Son of God." He then took the next step.

Be Baptized for the Forgiveness of Sins

Baptism is the moment where faith, repentance, and confession meet God's promise of salvation. In the waters of baptism, sins are washed away, the old life is buried, and a new life begins. Baptism is not just a symbol. Baptism is an act of obedient faith in which God performs the work of spiritual cleansing.

> **Acts 2:38** Repent and let every one of you be baptized in the name of Jesus Christ for the remission of sins.

> **Romans 6:4** Therefore we were buried with Him through baptism into death... that we also should walk in newness of life.

> **Mark 16:16** He who believes and is baptized will be saved.

Baptism unites the believer with the death, burial, and resurrection of Christ. It is the beginning of a transformed life—the moment when one becomes a new creation in Christ Jesus.

There is a lot of misinformation out there about what happens at baptism. Some go so far as saying it is not necessary to be saved. Some wait for months or even years to be baptized. What is the urgency if it is not connected to our salvation? In the Bible people who heard this teaching were baptized immediately. No one in the Bible questioned baptism like they do today. Let me summarize what the Bible says about the purpose of baptism with these 10 passages.

Read these for yourself.

- **Galatians 3:27** We are clothed with Christ.

- **Acts 22:16** Our sins are washed away.

- **Acts 2:38** We have received the forgiveness of sins and the gift of the Holy Spirit.

- **Romans 6:3-4** We are resurrected to begin our new life in Christ Jesus.

- **Romans 6:5** We are united with Christ and prepared for the final resurrection.
- **Romans 6:17-18** We are freed from sin and made servants of righteousness.

- **1 Corinthians 12:13; Acts 2:41; 47** We are added to the church, the body of the saved.

- **1 Peter 3:21** We are saved.

- **Colossians 2:11-12** We are spiritually circumcised, we are made people of God.

- **John 3:5** We are born again: of water and the Spirit.

If all these things happen at baptism, what happens if we are not baptized? It would seem logical to answer that none of these blessings will happen.

Ongoing Faithfulness

Salvation is not the end of the journey. Paul said in Romans 6 that we are raised from the grave, water baptism, to begin a new life. That new life must be lived until Jesus returns or until we go to meet him. God calls every Christian to live faithfully, to grow in grace, and to persevere until the end.

> **Revelation 2:10** Be faithful until death, and I will give you the crown of life.

The following chapters will deal with our faithful walk with Jesus after we are saved.

Suggested Reading

Muscle and a Shovel by Michael Shank

Baptism, Truths Beyond the Waters by Randy Short

Chapter 6
God's Plan for Your Life
(your time on Earth)

Galatians 2:20 I have been crucified with Christ. It is no longer I who live, but Christ who lives in me. And the life I now live in the flesh I live by faith in the Son of God, who loved me and gave himself for me.

Every believer will face trials, temptations, and hardships. We need to persevere through these. These moments refine our faith and prepare us for eternal reward.

> **James 1:12** Blessed is the man who remains steadfast under trial, for when he has stood the test he will receive the crown of life.

Perseverance through suffering proves the depth of one's faith. Faithfulness in hardship glorifies God and inspires others to remain strong.

Our time on Earth must be a time of faithfully following Jesus. That is true in whatever situation we find ourselves. The following verse of scripture speaks to us today, but it was first meant to speak to first century Christians who were undergoing terrible persecution. John, inspired by the Holy Spirit did not write that God was going to remove them from the terrible situation but rather that regardless of their situation they should remain faithful.

> **Revelation 2:10** Do not fear what you are about to suffer. Behold, the devil is about to throw some of you into prison, that you may be tested, and for ten days you will have tribulation. Be faithful unto death, and I will give you the crown of life.

The Bible clearly teaches that obedience and faith must continue throughout life. The Christian walk is a daily renewal of devotion, trust, and service. Remember when we mentioned under the heading of repentance what Jesus said about discipleship.

> **Luke 9:23** And he said to all, "If anyone would come after me, let him deny himself and take up his cross daily and follow me.

Faithfulness is a daily and lifelong struggle. We make mistakes and we sin, but we cannot give up. As we follow Him we are cleansed of our sins.

> **1 John 1:5** This is the message we have heard from him and proclaim to you, that God is light, and in him is no darkness at all. 6 If we say we have fellowship with him while we walk in darkness, we lie and do not practice the truth. 7 But if we walk in

the light, as he is in the light, we have fellowship with one another, and the blood of Jesus his Son cleanses us from all sin.

Faithfulness is not perfection. It includes an effort on our part to live perfectly as our perfect example Jesus Christ lived. Jesus knowing our frailties extended his mercy and grace to us and this passage says if we are sincerely trying "the blood of Jesus cleanses us from all sin." Not giving up is faithfulness.

Through prayer, worship, and study of God's word, the believer remains connected to the source of life, Jesus Christ Himself.

In this way, God's plan for your new life is not only about being saved from sin. It is about being transformed into the likeness of His Son, walking in the light, and living each day for His glory.

When a person is baptized into Christ and begins walking in newness of life, that moment marks not the end but the beginning of a lifelong journey. God's plan for your life on earth is a daily calling to live by faith, walk in love, and serve with purpose. The Christian life is a sacred partnership—God works within you, shaping your character and guiding your steps, while you commit yourself to living faithfully in His service.

The Bible teaches that living faithfully to Jesus and His church means a lifetime of loyalty, obedience, and spiritual growth. Faithfulness is not passive belief. It is a living, active devotion that shows itself in every part of one's life. It involves walking with Christ through joy and trial, trusting Him in every season, and allowing His Spirit to produce lasting fruit in your heart.

Faithfulness to Jesus

Following His Teachings and Commandments

Jesus made it clear that love for Him is shown through obedience. Faithful living flows from a heart that honors His word and seeks to put His teachings into daily practice.

> **John 14:23** If anyone loves Me, he will keep My word.

Jesus compared the wise person to one who builds their house on the rock—hearing and obeying His words ensures that when the storms of life come, faith stands firm.

> **Matthew 7:24** Everyone then who hears these words of mine and does them will be like a wise man who built his house on the rock. 25 And the

rain fell, and the floods came, and the winds blew and beat on that house, but it did not fall, because it had been founded on the rock.

Jesus goes on to preach about the opposite case. What happens when we hear but do not obey His words?

Matthew 7:26 And everyone who hears these words of mine and does not do them will be like a foolish man who built his house on the sand. 27 And the rain fell, and the floods came, and the winds blew and beat against that house, and it fell, and great was the fall of it.

Faithfulness is not perfection. It is persistence. It is choosing each day to follow Jesus' example and live by His truth and building our house on it.

Trusting in His Sovereignty

Faithful living also means trusting that God is in control, even when life is uncertain. The Christian's hope is anchored in the faithfulness of God Himself.

Hebrews 10:23 Let us hold fast the confession of our hope without wavering, for He who promised is faithful.

2 Timothy 2:13 If we are faithless, He remains faithful; He cannot deny Himself.

Our confidence rests not in our own strength but in God's unchanging nature. His promises to sustain us when our faith is tested.

Faithfulness to the Church

Commitment to Fellowship

The early church modeled a vibrant community of believers united in worship, teaching, and mutual care. Faithful Christians today are called to the same commitment.

> **Acts 2:42** They devoted themselves to the apostles' teaching and to fellowship, to the breaking of bread and to prayer.

> **Hebrews 10:24–25** Let us consider how to stir up one another to love and good works, not neglecting to meet together.

The church is not a place to attend. The church is a family to which one belongs. Regular fellowship strengthens faith and keeps the believer grounded in spiritual growth.

Unity and Service

Faithfulness within the body of Christ includes promoting unity, using spiritual gifts, and serving others with humility and love.

> **1 Corinthians 1:10** Paul urged the church to "be united in mind and judgment," calling believers to harmony rather than division.

> **Romans 12:4–5** For as in one body we have many members... so we, though many, are one body in Christ.

The church thrives when every member fulfills their purpose. Service, humility, and encouragement are practical expressions of faithfulness to God's people.

Bearing Fruit in Ministry

The evidence of a faithful life is fruitfulness. When believers live by the Spirit, their actions reflect the character of Christ and draw others to Him.

> **Galatians 5:22–23** The fruit of the Spirit is love, joy, peace, patience, kindness, goodness, faithfulness, gentleness, self-control.

Matthew 25:21 In the parable of the talents, the master says, "Well done, good and faithful servant." Faithfulness means using our gifts, time, and resources for God's purposes.

A faithful Christian does not simply believe—they serve, they love, and they grow.

Living by God's Pattern of Righteousness

The Christian way of life is rooted in a divine pattern—a moral and spiritual standard that reflects God's own nature. It is not a static list of rules, but a living expression of God's holiness, revealed through Jesus Christ and applied by the Holy Spirit.

Foundational Principles

Christian ethics begin with love. Jesus summarized all commandments in two great principles:

Matthew 22:37-39 Love the Lord your God with all your heart... and love your neighbor as yourself.

The Ten Commandments laid the foundation of moral law—honoring God, respecting others, and living justly. The prophets echoed this truth:

Micah 6:8 To act justly, to love mercy, and to walk humbly with your God.

Internal and Radical Ethics

Jesus raised the moral standard by addressing the heart, not just outward behavior. His teachings in the Sermon on the Mount, **Matthew 5-7**, reveal that righteousness begins within.

- Anger equals the spirit of murder (**Matthew 5:21-22**).

- Lust equals the seed of adultery (**Matthew 5:27-28**).

- The Golden Rule sums up all godly living. Do to others as you would have them do to you. (**Matthew 7:12**).

God's plan is not just for outward conformity, but for inward transformation.

The Role of the Holy Spirit

The Holy Spirit works within every believer to shape character and produce virtue.

Romans 12:2 Do not be conformed to this world but be transformed by the renewal of your mind.

Galatians 5:22–23 The Spirit's fruit replaces selfishness with love, anxiety with peace, and weakness with self-control.

Through the Spirit's power, the believer learns to reflect the heart of Christ.

Guidelines for a Life of Purpose

The Bible provides timeless guidance for daily living:

Sexual purity

Marriage should be honored by all, and the marriage bed kept pure **Hebrews 13:4.**

Stewardship

Each of you should use whatever gift you have received to serve others. **1 Peter 4:10.**

Honesty

The Lord detests lying lips, but He delights in those who are truthful. **Proverbs 12:22.**

Forgiveness

> Forgive us our debts, as we forgive our debtors. **Matthew 6:12**

Living faithfully means allowing every aspect of life—relationships, work, speech, and thought—to glorify God.

The Goal of a Faithful Life

The Christian life is a journey of growth, endurance, and hope. It is a life lived in gratitude for the grace of God and in anticipation of the eternal reward He has promised.

Paul's words in **Galatians 2:20** remind us that our lives no longer belong to ourselves; we belong to Christ. And the voice of Jesus in Revelation calls us to hold fast until the end:

> Be faithful unto death, and I will give you the crown of life. **Revelation 2:10**

Every faithful moment, every act of love, every trial endured in faith, moves us closer to that crown. God's plan for your life on earth is simple yet profound—to walk with Christ, serve His people, and bring glory to His name until the day you see Him face to face.

Jesus had a successful life. He knew that he would have to sacrifice much for that to happen. This is how He put it

> Truly, truly, I say to you, unless a grain of wheat falls into the earth and dies, it remains alone; but if it dies, it bears much fruit. Whoever loves his life loses it, and whoever hates his life in this world will keep it for eternal life. If anyone serves me, he must follow me; and where I am, there will my servant be also. If anyone serves me, the Father will honor him. **John 12:24-26**

Jesus was certainly talking about his on sacrifice on the cross when he used the analogy of a seed of wheat falling to the earth and dying. He knew his sacrifice was necessary to bear much fruit or be successful. Indeed, Jesus is still bearing fruit today. While this was a prediction of his coming death it was also a message for all His disciples, those present with them and for us today.

The next part starts with the word "Whoever" and indicated that the message is broader than the immediate application to Jesus. I would also say that it is to sacrifice time, money and effort but not necessarily death. Sacrifice is necessary for anything in our lives to be successful. Every successful business owner knows how much sacrifice it takes. Do you want to be a successful wife or husband? It takes sacrifice. It requires sacrifice to be a fruitful employee. Do you want to be a successful mother? Tell a soon to be mother in the middle of her gestation about sacrifice! Then there is the pain and labor of giving birth. Mothers, getting up every two hours during the night to care for their newborn, understand the necessity of sacrifice.

To be a successful follower of Jesus Christ you must be ready to make sacrifices. God wants us to be successful, and he gives us the formula to achieve it.

"Unless a grain of wheat falls into the earth and dies, it remains alone; but if it dies, it bears much fruit."

"It is an attribute of greatness and of American exceptionalism to not surrender to our nature, ... no matter the personal cost." Charlie Kirk

Church Participation

Participating in the assemblies of the church is so important. I have heard Christians say I can be a Christian without participating in the church. Really? The world is a tough place. There are many temptations and difficulties. When it comes to living the life talked about in this chapter the church is there to help.

The New Testament is mostly about the church. It begins with begins with Jesus' promise to build His church in **Matthew 16:18**. The Acts of the Apostles and the numerous epistles were written to or about local churches. The Greek word ekklesia is translated church. The word church appears 76 to 118 times in the New Testament depending on the translation you use. To say the church is unimportant or that you can lead the Christian life without the church denies Scriptures and what Jesus did.

> **Acts 20:28** Pay careful attention to yourselves and to all the flock, in which the Holy Spirit has made you overseers, to care for the church of God, which he obtained with his own blood.

The Hebrew writer also had something to say about church attendance. Some Christians had stopped attending services and he condemns this attitude.

> **Hebrews 10:24** And let us consider how to stir up one another to love and good works, 25 not neglecting to meet together, as is the habit of some, but encouraging one another, and all the more as you see the Day drawing near.

The songs we sing, the prayers we send up to God, the Lord's Supper we take, the moment of giving and the study and preaching from the Bible in an assembly of likeminded believers serve to build us up to face the difficulties and temptations the work puts on us daily. Do not miss getting involved in a true Bible believing church. If you are serious about your Christianity, you will want to know more about the church as detailed in the Bible.

Suggested Reading

Churches in the Shape of Scripture by Dan Chambers

The Church of Christ, by Edward C. Wharton

Chapter 7
God's Plan for the Afterlife
(eternal home)

John 14:2 In my Father's house are many rooms. If it were not so, would I have told you that I go to prepare a place for you? And if I go and prepare a place for you, I will come again and will take you to myself, that where I am you may be also.

"No one truly knows who makes it to heaven but God. Only God knows an individual's heart. We only have discernment by a person's words and actions." Charlie Kirk

From the beginning of creation to the end of time, God's plan has always been about fellowship with His people. Life on earth is not the end of our story—it is the prelude to eternity. Every soul that walks this earth is moving toward an eternal destination, and Scripture makes clear that eternity holds only two final outcomes: eternal life with God or eternal separation from Him.

The afterlife is not an abstract idea or a distant mystery; it is the final fulfillment of God's redemptive plan. For the believer, it is the moment when faith becomes sight and hope becomes reality. For the unbeliever, it is the tragic confirmation of a life lived apart from the Savior.

For the Believer - The Hope of Glory

The Bible paints a picture of eternity that is both comforting and glorious for those who belong to Christ. It is not a life of floating spirits or endless clouds, but a renewed creation where heaven and earth are united, and God dwells with His redeemed forever.

At Death With Christ in Paradise

A spiritual dwelling

Death for the Christian is not the end but the doorway to a greater life. Paul declared:

> **2 Corinthians 5:8** Yes, we are of good courage, and we would rather be away from the body and at home with the Lord.

The believer's spirit immediately enters the presence of Christ, safe and at peace.

Paradise

Jesus told the repentant thief:

> Truly, I say to you, today you will be with me in paradise. **Luke 23:43**

This reminds us that even before the final resurrection, there is conscious joy and communion with God. It is a foretaste of the eternal glory yet to come.

After death nothing more awaits except the judgment.

Hebrews 9:27 And just as it is appointed for man to die once, and after that comes judgment,

We must make the most of this life to prepare for the next. That is what Lazarus did in the worst of circumstances.

He was a beggar and covered in sores. He had no hope in this present life, but he was prepared for Paradise. Paradise in this text and in the Jewish context was to be united with Abraham in the afterlife and that is exactly what happened. The rich man in the story was selfish and unwilling to help better the lives of his fellow man. Lazarus had laid at his gate hoping for the crumbs that fell from the rich man's table. Lazarus dies and the angels carried him away to Abraham's bosom. The rich man also died, and he opened his eyes in torment.

Luke 16:22 The poor man died and was carried by the angels to Abraham's side. The rich man also died and was buried, 23 and in Hades, being in torment, he lifted his eyes and saw Abraham far off and Lazarus at his side.

The rich man wants comfort, but Abraham says that is impossible. He then wants Abraham to send Lazarus back to the living so he can tell his brothers to change their lives and not come to this place of torment.

Abraham says that is also impossible and then adds:

> **Luke 16:29** ... They have Moses and the Prophets; let them hear them.' 30 And he said, 'No, father Abraham, but if someone goes to them from the dead, they will repent.' 31 He said to him, 'If they do not hear Moses and the Prophets, neither will they be convinced if someone should rise from the dead.'

Moses and the prophets here mean the Scriptures of Moses and the Prophets. In other word, if they will not listen to what God says through His scriptures they will not listen to a dead man returned to life either.

How important is it that we listen and conform to what God has spoken in His Word, the Bible.

We also learn that people recognize people in the afterlife. We will continue to be who we are in this life when we die.

We also learn that there is an immediate judgment much the way someone accused of a crime today will be put in jail though the final judgment has not yet been rendered.

The Bible speaks of a final judgment when Jesus returns

> **Acts 17:31** because he has fixed a day on which he will judge the world in righteousness by a man whom he has appointed; and of this he has given assurance to all by raising him from the dead.

Jesus said:

> **John 12:48** The one who rejects me and does not receive my words has a judge; the word that I have spoken will judge him on the last day.

There is a last day coming. There is a judgment day coming. To be ready you must receive Jesus words and live by them.

Christians have no reason to fear that day. Look at what the apostle Paul said:

> **Romans 8:1** There is therefore now no condemnation for those who are in Christ Jesus. 2 For the law of the Spirit of life has set you free in Christ Jesus from the law of sin and death.

At Jesus's Return: Resurrection and New Creation

The first resurrection

When Christ returns, He will call His people from their graves. The dead in Christ will rise first, and those who are alive will be transformed in an instant.

1 Thessalonians 4:16 For the Lord himself will descend from heaven with a cry of command, with the voice of an archangel, and with the sound of the trumpet of God. And the dead in Christ will rise first. 17 Then we who are alive, who are left, will be caught up together with them in the clouds to meet the Lord in the air, and so we will always be with the Lord.

Jesus set the judgment scene in **Matthew 25.**

Matthew 25:31 When the Son of Man comes in his glory, and all the angels with him, then he will sit on his glorious throne. 32 Before him will be gathered all the nations, and he will separate people one from another as a shepherd separates the sheep from the goats. 33 And he will place the sheep on his right, but the goats on the left. 34 Then the King will say to those on his right, 'Come, you who are blessed by my Father, inherit the kingdom prepared for you from the foundation of the world... 46 And these [those on the left] will go away into eternal punishment, but the righteous into eternal life.

A glimpse of eternal life for those who are saved:

> **Revelation 21:3** And I heard a loud voice from the throne saying, "Behold, the dwelling place of God is with man. He will dwell with them, and they will be his people, and God himself will be with them as their God. 4 He will wipe away every tear from their eyes, and death shall be no more, neither shall there be mourning, nor crying, nor pain anymore, for the former things have passed away.

That afterlife is described as a world where there is no more death, sorrow, or pain. God Himself will dwell with His people in perfect peace, and eternity will be a place of joy, worship, and everlasting fellowship.

Specific things we will be doing are not detailed in the Scriptures, but we can trust in God that it will be wonderful. Paul was taken up to heaven, and this is what he said about that experience.

> **2 Corinthians 12:2** I know a man in Christ who fourteen years ago was caught up to the third heaven—whether in the body or out of the body I do not know, God knows. 3 And I know that this man was caught up into paradise—whether in the body or out of the body I do not know, God

knows— 4 and he heard things that cannot be told, which man may not utter.

Paul was not allowed to give details about what he saw. But it was marvelous things. Earlier he had written to the Corinthians saying:

> **1 Corinthians 2:9** But, as it is written What no eye has seen, nor ear heard, nor the heart of man imagined, what God has prepared for those who love him.

For the Unrighteous: The Reality of Judgment

While the believer's eternity is filled with light and hope, Scripture also speaks soberly about the destiny of those who reject God's grace. The same Bible that reveals heaven also warns of eternal separation for those who refuse to follow Christ.

I heard a story about a sociology teacher in a major university. One day he asked his large class how many believed in heaven. Almost all raised their hands. He then followed up by asking how many believed in hell and no one raised their hand.

Hell is not a place we like to talk about, but Jesus certainly did and used it to motivate people to turn their lives over to him. You might be surprised to know that in the Bible Jesus is the one who spoke more about hell than any other. This is not a comprehensive run down of all the passages but if this is a new thought to you might should do more Bible reading on this subject. This table is a summary of what Jesus taught.

Category	Common Phrases Used by Jesus	Key References
Explicit "hell" (Gehenna)	fire of hell, body and soul destroyed	Matt 5:22–30; 10:28; Mark 9:43–48; Luke 12:5
Fire imagery	eternal fire, fiery furnace	Matt 13:40–42; 25:41
Darkness imagery	outer darkness, weeping and gnashing of teeth	Matt 8:12; 22:13; 25:30
Judgment imagery	separation, condemnation, punishment	Matt 13:49–50; John 5:28–29
Hades / torment imagery	flames, thirst, anguish	Luke 16:19–31

At the End of the Age: Final Judgment and Condemnation

Look at what Jesus said.

John 5:28 Do not marvel at this, for an hour is coming when all who are in the tombs will hear his voice 29 and come out, those who have done good to the resurrection of life, and those who have done evil to the resurrection of judgment.

The apostle John speaks of the judgment scene in his book. The final verdict will go something like this.

Revelation 20:11 Then I saw a great white throne and him who was seated on it. From his presence earth and sky fled away, and no place was found for them. 12 And I saw the dead, great and small, standing before the throne, and books were opened. Then another book was opened, which is the book of life. And the dead were judged by what was written in the books, according to what they had done. 13 And the sea gave up the dead who were in it, Death and Hades gave up the dead who were in them, and they were judged, each one of them, according to what they had done. 14 Then Death and Hades were thrown into the lake of fire. This is the second death, the lake of fire. 15 And if anyone's name was not found written in the book of life, he was thrown into the lake of fire.

John describes the great white throne judgment, where every person stands before God. Those whose names are not written in the Book of Life are cast into the lake of fire—the "second death."

Eternal separation from God

This eternal punishment is not annihilation but separation—the ultimate tragedy of rejecting God's offer of salvation. It is the fulfillment of the choice to live apart from Him forever.

> **2 Thessalonians 1:7** ... when the Lord Jesus is revealed from heaven with his mighty angels 8 in flaming fire, inflicting vengeance on those who do not know God and on those who do not obey the gospel of our Lord Jesus. 9 They will suffer the punishment of eternal destruction, away from the presence of the Lord and from the glory of his might.

Those who do not know God and who do not obey the gospel of our Lord Jesus will be eternally separated from the presence of the Lord in flaming fire.

The Final State: Eternal Life or Eternal Separation

God's plan for the afterlife is a plan of perfect justice and perfect love. Every human being will stand before their Creator. For the redeemed, eternity will be life in a glorified body, in a perfected universe, worshiping the Lamb forever. For those who reject Christ, it will be eternal separation from His presence.

Heaven and hell are not merely destinations. They are the results of our relationship with God or a rejection of it. The invitation of Jesus remains open to all.

> **Matthew 11:28** Come to me, all who labor and are heavy laden, and I will give you rest.

The church and the Spirt say come.

> **Revelation 22:17** The Spirit and the Bride say, "Come." And let the one who hears say, "Come." And let the one who is thirsty come; let the one who desires take the water of life without price.

Eternity is certain. The question is not whether you will live forever—but where you will live. God's plan for your afterlife is not meant to fill you with fear, but with hope, because He has gone to prepare a place for you.

> **John 14:1** Let not your hearts be troubled. Believe in God; believe also in me. 2 In my Father's house

are many rooms. If it were not so, would I have told you that I go to prepare a place for you? 3 And if I go and prepare a place for you, I will come again and will take you to myself, that where I am you may be also.

The door to that eternal home stands open for all who believe and follow Him.

Chapter 8

Atomic Christianity

1 Thessalonians 1:7 So that you became an example to all the believers in Macedonia and in Achaia.

"I am far more interested in what God wants from me than what I want from God." Charlie Kirk

"What God wants from me is a life fighting for truth." Charlie Kirk

The phrase "Atomic Christianity" is a metaphor for the extraordinary, radiating influence a believer can have in the world. Just as the atom contains incredible energy that can transform matter, a Christian filled with the Holy Spirit carries immense potential to transform lives through love, service, and hope. This is not a passive faith but a vibrant, active force that touches everyone around us.

Jesus called it light. It would radiate to a World lost in sin.

> **Matthew 5:14** You are the light of the world. A city set on a hill cannot be hidden. 15 Nor do people light a lamp and put it under a basket, but on a stand, and it gives light to all in the house. 16 In the same way, let your light shine before others, so that they may see your good works and give glory to your Father who is in heaven.

Good works! Love can be seen through good works.

Atomic Christianity Radiates Love

Love is at the core of the Christian life. Jesus made it clear that loving God and loving others is the essence of all spiritual obedience.

Love God fully

> **Matthew 22:37** And he said to him, "You shall love the Lord your God with all your heart and with all your soul and with all your mind.

Loving God is demonstrated through obedience to His Word:

> **John 14:15** If you love me, you will keep my commandments.

Love your neighbor

Jesus also instructed us:

> **Matthew 22:39...** You shall love your neighbor as yourself.

The parable of the Good Samaritan, Luke 10:29-37, shows that love is active. It requires being aware of those in need. It requires offering help to those in need. At time it will require making personal sacrifices.

Love your family

Love is also expressed in family relationships through honor and respect.

> **Matthew 19:19** Honor your father and mother, and You shall love your neighbor as yourself.

Jesus calls loving out parents as honoring our parents.

> **Ephesians 5:33** However, let each one of you love his wife as himself, and let the wife see that she respects her husband.

Paul says a wife's love for her husband is expressed in respect.

Love even your enemies

Love is not limited to neighbors, friends, and family. Jesus challenges us to love those who oppose us:

> **Matthew 5:44** But I say to you, Love your enemies and pray for those who persecute you,

Loving your enemies is tough but it is what Jesus wants. Loving and praying for those who persecute you may be even tougher, but Jesus was able to do just that, and we are His followers. Listen to Jesus modelling this radical love from the cross.

> **Luke 23:34** And Jesus said, "Father, forgive them, for they know not what they do." And they cast lots to divide his garments.

Atomic Christianity spreads this love in all directions. Like energy radiating outward, it reaches people we know and those we have never met, touching lives with God's compassion.

Atomic Christianity Radiates Through Service

Faith is active. Love without action is incomplete, and Atomic Christianity channels love into practical service:

Serving others

In **Matthew 25:40** Jesus reminds us:

> And the King will answer them, 'Truly, I say to you, as you did it to one of the least of these my brothers, you did it to me.'

Each act of kindness and service, no matter how small, spreads God's influence in the world.

Using spiritual gifts

> **1 Peter 4:10** As each has received a gift, use it to serve one another, as good stewards of God's varied grace:

Peter calls believers to serve one another using our God-given gifts. Service radiates outward like light, encouraging others and strengthening the body of Christ.

Atomic Christianity Radiates Hope

Hope is positive about the future. Hope is the spiritual energy that motivates and uplifts. It is rooted in the promise of Jesus' resurrection and the assurance of eternal life:

Confident hope

> **Romans 15:13** May the God of hope fill you with all joy and peace in believing, so that by the power of the Holy Spirit you may abound in hope.

A guiding light

Just as light from a lamp guides travelers in darkness, the hope of Christ illuminates lives, inspiring those around us to trust in God's promises and to see the good beyond the present distress.

Atomic Christianity Influences All Around You

The power of this faith is natural, pervasive, and unavoidable. Atomic Christianity is not a destructive force, but rather a transforming one. Just as atomic energy spreads so the love, service, and hope of a believer spreads.

A contagious faith

It is like yeast working through dough.

> **Matthew 13:33** He told them another parable. 'The kingdom of heaven is like leaven that a woman took and hid in three measures of flour, till it was all leavened.'

A faithful life permeates families, communities, nations, and even entire generations.

An invitation to participate.

Every Christian is called to this dynamic influence. Faith is not meant to remain private; it radiates outward when we live fully for God. It is as Christian circles call it, evangelistic.

Be a Part of Atomic Christianity

God invites you to embrace your role as a radiant source of His love, hope, and service. Each action, word, and thought infused with faith is part of the "energy" of Atomic Christianity.

Live intentionally

Seek ways to share God's love and hope daily.

Serve generously

Let acts of service be a visible reflection of Christ's heart.

Remain steadfast

Allow your faith to radiate consistently, even in the face of challenges.

> "Courage is contagious, and when one person stands up, others are emboldened." Charlie Kirk

Atomic Christianity is not about physical power or force. It is about the transformative influence of a life surrendered to God. Like an atom's energy released, your faith has the potential to touch countless lives, creating ripple effects of goodness, mercy, and hope that extend far beyond what you can see.

My prayer is that this book will point you to God's Word, the Bible and help you to be an atomic Christian, radiating to all those around you the Good News of Jesus Christ.

Contact with the author:
Randy.kathyshort@gmail.com

Made in the USA
Columbia, SC
19 January 2026

77187659R00062